My Mind is My Masterpiece

By Nekita Shelton

Copyright© Page

MY MIND IS MY MASTERPIECE
By Nekita Shelton

Dedication page

Dedicated to the confident girl hiding behind her thoughts, ideas and intelligence. She is timid at times, yet full of hidden potential and possibilities.

In the morning when I pray, I hear God say my mind is beautiful;

I hear him say I am smart, I am brave and that my mind is my best tool.

He surrounds my thoughts with positivity, so that I may rise and be my best me.

As I open my eyes, feet to the floor, I get so excited for what my mind has in store.

I brush my teeth and wash my face;

Preparing to speak my affirmations with grace.

Say it with me, "I am a brown girl created and uniquely designed, with purpose to achieve;

I am a girl that will let my heart and my knowledge lead"

I was made to walk, talk and think differently;

Not like my friends or family, but like me.

I am a girl that will not hide behind my thoughts, but will embrace them.

When I enter a room, I will not be afraid,

Instead I will tell myself I am confident and wonderfully made.

I will hold my head high without doubt or shame, because being myself is my one true aim.

I will replace "I think" with "I can",

Because being bold and courageous
is in high demand.

I will push myself until the race is won;

I will remember to laugh, be grateful, and just have fun.

Getting good grades is an honor to receive.

Making myself and my parents proud
is easy when I believe.

I will use my mind as a guide, to stand up for what is right; Even when the world puts up a fight.

Putting my best foot forth is the key,

Because my only competition is me.

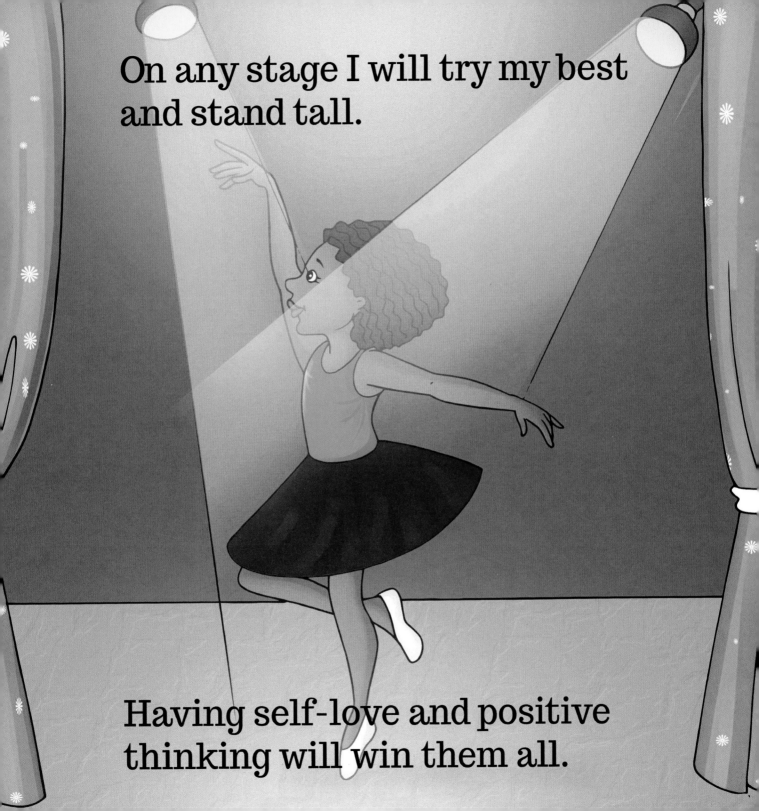

On any stage I will try my best and stand tall.

Having self-love and positive thinking will win them all.

My vision of me is special, you see;

My mind is my Masterpiece, fit for a queen like me.